Discovery KIDS

Spin-the-Wheel Incredible Animals

LIVE. LEARN. DISCOVER.

Parragon

Bath · New York · Singapore · Hong Kong · Cologne · Delhi · Melbourne

Aardvark True or False

Answer the questions and put a check in the correct box.

a. The name *aardvark* means "earth-pig."

True ☑ False ☐

b. The aardvark is a nocturnal animal.

True ☐ False ☐

DiscoveryFact™

An aardvark's sticky tongue can be up to 12 inches long to help it lick termites from a termite mound. It can also close its nostrils to keep out soil and insects.

Spot the Difference

Can you find five differences between the two aardvark pictures?

Wheel Quiz:

What is the aardvark's favorite food?

a. Termites
b. Truffles
c. Tortillas

African Elephant

Word Scramble

Unscramble the letters in each word to discover an interesting fact about the African elephant.

SKUTS
UKTNR
YVOIR

The elephant has two TUSKS on either side of its TRUNK. These are made of IVORY.

Label the Picture

Fill in the correct words to label the picture.

DiscoveryFact™

The elephant flaps its large ears to keep cool. It will use its trunk to cover itself with dust to protect its thick skin from the sun.

MOUTH
TUSK
EYE
TRUNK
EAR
FOOT

Wheel Quiz:

How tall can an African elephant grow?

a. 15 feet
b. 9 feet
c. 10–12 feet

Odd One Out

Take a close look at the top picture.
Which picture below is the odd one out?
Put a check in the box next to it.

DiscoveryFact™

The cheetah is the fastest animal on land, running at speeds of up to 75 miles per hour.

Word Scramble

Unscramble the letters in each word below to discover an interesting fact about the cheetah.

A cheetah can go without OFOD Food for up to UORF four days.

Wheel Quiz:

What is the endangered status of the cheetah?

a. High
b. Medium
c. Low

Giraffe

Close-Up Challenge

Using the list, write which part of the giraffe is shown in the picture.

KNEE
TAIL
HORNS
NECK

1

neck

2

HORNS

3

tail

4

knee

What Does It Mean?

Giraffes belong to a group of animals called even-toed ungulates. But can you guess what *ungulate* means? Circle the right answer.

a. Hoofed animal
b. Two-toed animal
c. Four-footed animal

DiscoveryFact™

The giraffe's blue-black tongue is up to 20 inches long. It's tough enough to pull down thorny shrubs.

Wheel Quiz:

How tall is a giraffe?

a. 8–10 feet tall
b. 11–13 feet tall
c. 14–17 feet tall

Lion Maze

The lion cub is lost in the tall grass. Help the cub find her way to her mom.

Start

Finish

Hidden Food

Wildebeest are the lion's favorite food. How many wildebeest can you find on the page?

DiscoveryFact™

The lion is the only member of the cat family that lives in a group, called a pride. The females of the pride hunt together.

Wheel Quiz:

What do lions eat?

a. Antelopes and gazelles
b. Warthogs and buffalo
c. All of the above

Wildebeest Math

Do the math to find out some interesting facts about the wildebeest.

1. How many wildebeest make the great migration each year?
3.5 + 2.5 – 4.5: ___
Answer: ___ million

2. How far do the wildebeest travel?
1,247 + 621 – 68: ___
Answer: ___ miles

3. How many months does the migration take?
24 + 6 – 18: ___
Answer: ___ months

DiscoveryFact™

Wildebeest make a long migration every year to find new feeding grounds during times of drought.

Wildebeest Herd

Draw your own wildebeest herd in the space below.

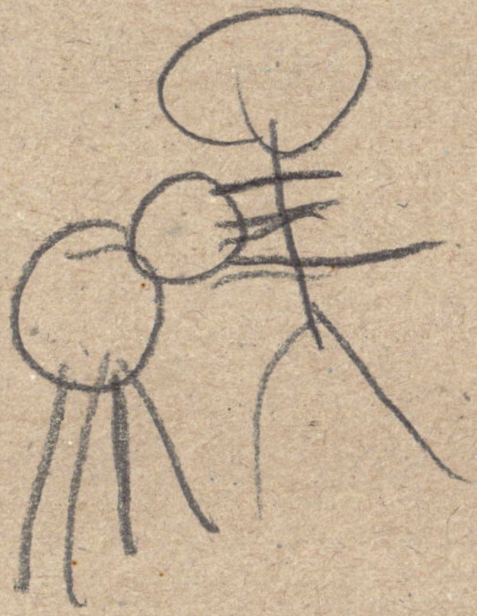

Wheel Quiz:

Where do blue wildebeest live?

a. South and East Africa
b. South and East Asia
c. South and East Australia

Plains Zebra

Find the difference

Can you find four differences between the two pictures below?

DiscoveryFact™

No two zebras have exactly the same striped pattern—each one is unique.

Zebra Shadow

Which of these shadows matches the zebra?

Wheel Quiz:

What is the plains zebra's endangered status?

a. High
b. Medium
c. Low

DiscoveryFact™

Although it can't fly, the emu can run at 31 miles per hour. To outrun an enemy, it zigzags until the hunter is exhausted.

Emu Hidden Fact

Cross out the numbers in the table below, then copy the remaining letters into the boxes to discover a special fact about the emu.

4	E	6	G	4	G	B	L	7	A	2	C	3	K	G	R	9	E	8
E	N	3	6	7	S	3	H	E	6	3	L	8	L	T	H	2	3	4
7	7	I	2	9	2	1	9	6	8	4	5	6	C	5	4	3	K	2

The emu's _ _ _ varies in color from _ _ _ _ _ _ to dark _ _ _ _ _ _. The _ _ _ _ _ _ is very _ _ _ _ _ _.

Flightless Bird

Draw your own bird that doesn't fly based on the emu.

Wheel Quiz:

How tall is the emu?

a. Up to 8 inches
b. Up to 3 feet
c. Up to 6.6 feet

Red Kangaroo

What Does It Mean?

Kangaroos belong to a group of animals called marsupials. But can you guess what *marsupial* means? Check the box next to the right answer.

- ☐ a. An animal with a pouch
- ☐ b. An animal with a tail
- ☐ c. An animal with long feet

Clue, look carefully at the belly.

Match the kangaroo

Look at the picture below. Then circle the shadow that matches the picture exactly.

DiscoveryFact™

The red kangaroo is the largest kangaroo. It can jump 30 feet in one leap.

Wheel Quiz:

What does the red kangaroo eat?

a. Grass and leaves
b. Insects
c. Small mammals

Word Maze

Work your way through the maze below by coloring in the words: "AUSTRALIAN MARSUPIAL."

Wombat Shadow

Look at the picture above. Then circle the shadow that matches the picture exactly.

DiscoveryFact™

Wombats are native only to Australia but most Australians have never seen a wild wombat.

Wheel Quiz:

What do wombats eat?

a. Small rodents
b. Grass and roots
c. Insects and grubs

Quiz

How much do you know about these animals? Try this quiz, then use your wheel to check your answers.

1. Which is tallest?
   a. African lion
   b. Blue wildebeest
   c. Plains zebra

2. What animal is up to 10 inches tall?
   a. Emu
   b. Aardvark
   c. Burrowing owl

3. Which of these animals is found only in Australia?
   a. Wild dog
   b. Burrowing owl
   c. Wombat

4. Which animal eats only grass?
   a. Blue wildebeest
   b. Elephant
   c. Aardvark

5. What eats gazelle and springbok?
a. Rattlesnake
b. Cheetah
c. Pronghorn

6. How tall can an African elephant grow up to?
a. 6 feet
b. 12 feet
c. 15 feet

7. Which animal is found in North America?
a. Plains zebra
b. Bison
c. Red kangaroo

8. Which animal would you find in South America?
a. Armadillo
b. Aardvark
c. Pronghorn

9. Which is shortest?
a. Burrowing owl
b. Wombat
c. Aardvark

10. What is the endangered status of the burrowing owl?
a. High
b. Medium
c. Low

Pronghorn

Pronghorn

Code Breaker

Use the code breaker to crack the code, then write the answer in the space below.

A	B	C	D	E	F	G	H	I	J	K	L	M

N	O	P	Q	R	S	T	U	V	Y	X	Y	Z

Spot the Difference

DiscoveryFact™

The pronghorn is the second fastest land mammal in the world, after the cheetah.

Can you find five differences between these two pronghorns?

Wheel Quiz:

Where can you find the pronghorn?

a. Northern Europe
b. North Africa
c. North America

Bison Shadow

Look at the picture of the bison. Circle the shadow that matches the picture exactly.

Label the Picture

Fill in the correct words to label the picture.

NOSE
MOUTH
HORN
HOOF
EYE

DiscoveryFact™

Bison like to wallow in mud or dust. It probably helps get rid of ticks and lice from its thick, hairy coat, and might even keep it cool.

Wheel Quiz:

How big can bison grow?

a. Up to 8 feet
b. Up to 11.5 feet
c. Up to 15 feet

Burrowing Owl

Word Search

There are ten favorite burrowing owl foods hidden in the squares below. Can you find them all?

- CRICKET
- EARWIG
- MOUSE
- VOLE
- SHREW
- FROG
- LIZARD
- TOAD
- FRUIT
- PRAIRIE DOG

C	W	W	T	V	Q	A	C	S	C	P
V	R	G	M	Z	M	J	W	R	Y	R
H	T	I	A	V	O	L	E	R	W	A
G	I	W	C	A	U	F	R	O	G	I
G	L	R	A	K	S	J	H	L	J	R
R	I	A	I	D	E	D	S	L	Y	I
U	Z	E	L	Y	F	T	C	R	X	E
O	A	W	S	F	D	O	A	F	E	D
N	R	E	G	H	K	A	T	R	H	O
D	D	Y	P	Y	R	D	H	Q	H	G
F	R	U	I	T	X	T	U	S	T	B

Calculator Code

Crack the number code to finish the sentence.

1	2	3	4	5	6	7	8	9	10	11
C	D	E	G	H	N	O	R	S	U	W

The burrowing owl lines its nest with
5 7 8 9 3 or 1 7 11   2 10 6 4
_ _ _ _ _   _ _ _   _ _ _ _
which attracts insects to eat.

DiscoveryFact™
The burrowing owl nests in a hole in the ground. It can dig its own burrow, but will use empty burrows left by other animals.

Wheel Quiz:
What is the burrowing owl's endangered status?

a. High
b. Medium
c. Low

Prairie Dog Maze

This golden eagle has spotted the prairie dogs. Help them escape throug the maze to safety.

Hidden Food

Grasshoppers are the prairie dog's favorite snack. How many grasshoppers can you find on the page?

DiscoveryFact™

Prairie dogs live in burrows, with different rooms for sleeping, and many entrances and exits for safety.

Wheel Quiz:

What does the prairie dog eat?

a. Grass and insects
b. Birds and cats
c. Sheep and cattle

Greater Prairie Chicken

Take a look at this picture below. Then fill in the correct numbers to label the greater prairie chicken.

Close-Up

1. Crest
2. Beak
3. Eye
4. Throat sac
5. Foot
6. Tail
7. Wing

How Many?

Snakes will raid the prairie chicken's nest and eat its eggs. How many snakes can you count?

DiscoveryFact™

To attract a mate, the male prairie chicken puffs out the orange sacs on the side of its neck and slaps its tail.

Wheel Quiz:

What is the prairie chicken's endangered status?

a. High
b. Medium
c. Low

Prairie Rattlesnake

Odd One Out

Take a close look at the rattlesnakes below. One in each row is different. Put a check next to each rattlesnake that is different.

a

b

c

a

b

c

Sneaky Snake

There are 30 different species of rattlesnake. Draw your own rattlesnake in the space below.

DiscoveryFact™

Rattlesnakes give birth to live young (5 to 20 at a time). They do not lay eggs like most North American snakes.

Wheel Quiz:

How long is a prairie rattlesnake?

a. Up to 8 inches
b. Up to 24 inches
c. Up to 4 feet

Wild Dog Maze

This wild dog has been separated from his pack while hunting. Help him find his way back by completing this tricky maze!

Start

Finish

Spot the Difference

Can you find five differences between these African wild dogs?

DiscoveryFact™

Wild dogs hunt in packs. They attack together to overcome much bigger animals, such as zebras.

Wheel Quiz:

What do African wild dogs eat?

a. Cacti, shrubs
b. Grass
c. Wildebeest, zebra, antelope

Follow the Trail

The armadillo is trying to escape from the puma. Which trail will lead it to safety?

Label the Picture

Fill in the correct words to label the picture.

SNOUT
EARS
TAIL
CLAW

DiscoveryFact™

The armadillo can roll into a ball to protect itself. Its tough, leathery shell acts like armor.

Wheel Quiz:

What is the armadillo's endangered status?

a. High
b. Medium
c. Low

Code Breaker

Crack the number code below to discover some interesting facts about the cougar.

1	2	3	4	5	6	7	8	9	10	11	12	13
A	B	C	D	E	F	G	H	I	J	K	L	M

14	15	16	17	18	19	20	21	22	23	24	25	26
N	O	P	Q	R	S	T	U	V	W	X	Y	Z

2 15 18 14 / 3 21 2

When it is _ _ _ _, a cougar _ _ _

19 16 15 20 20 5 4

has a _ _ _ _ _ _ _ coat,

6 1 4 5 19

which _ _ _ _ _

19 9 24

after _ _ _ months.

Spot the Difference

Can you find five differences between these two cougars?

DiscoveryFact™

The cougar holds the record for the number of names it is known by. These include puma, mountain lion, and panther.

Wheel Quiz:

How long can a cougar be?

a. Up to 10 feet
b. Up to 8 feet
c. Up to 5 feet

Shadows

Only one of these shadows belongs to the hyena. Draw a circle around the right one.

Hidden Message

Cross out the numbers and the capital letters below. Write all the small letters that are left out in the spaces underneath to reveal where hyenas come from.

D	B	E	6	3	4	a	S	B	E	D	7	D	f	U	Y	G	r	6
C	D	S	7	D	S	i	B	E	S	D	I	7	C	c	S	B	a	E

DiscoveryFact™

Hyenas are so tough, they can crush the bones of their prey with their strong teeth so they can be digested.

Wheel Quiz:

What is the hyenas endangered status?

a. High
b. Medium
c. Low

Word Search

Can you find these words hidden in the squares below? They are all types of food eaten by incredible animals.

W	I	L	D	E	B	E	E	S	T	X
S	H	O	O	T	S	S	A	B	E	B
C	A	C	T	I	S	S	S	D	R	R
C	A	C	Y	W	I	A	W	F	M	T
L	H	T	H	R	G	R	E	G	I	Y
E	L	L	E	Z	A	G	R	H	T	U
A	E	R	T	Y	Y	D	T	J	E	I
V	F	Z	E	B	R	A	Y	K	S	O
E	L	K	O	P	O	I	U	M	N	P
S	K	N	R	T	I	U	R	F	U	C
A	N	T	E	L	O	P	E	B	V	C

CACTI
WILDEBEEST
ANTELOPE
TERMITES
FRUIT
SHOOTS
GRASS
GAZELLE
LEAVES
ZEBRA

Animal Food

Can you match the food with the animals that eat it?

Cougar

Giraffe

Cacti

Wild dog

Seed pods

Acacia leaves

Zebra

African elephant

Deer

Pronghorn

ANSWERS

Page 2
Aardvark True or False
a. True, it is an Afrikaans word
b. True

Page 3

Wheel Quiz:
a. Termites

Page 4
Word Scramble
The elephant has two tusks on either side of its trunk. These are made of ivory.

Page 5
Label the Picture

Wheel Quiz
c. 10–12 feet tall.

Page 6
Odd One Out

Page 7
Word Scramble
A cheetah can go without food for up to four days.

Wheel quiz:
b. Medium

Page 8
Close-Up Challenge
1. Neck
2. Horns
3. Tail
4. Knee

Page 9
What Does It Mean?
a. Hoofed animal.

Wheel Quiz
c. 14–17 feet tall

Page 10
Lion Maze

Page 11
Hidden Food
12 Wildebeest

Wheel Quiz
c. All of the above.

Page 12
Wildebeest Math
1. 1.5 million
2. 1,800 miles
3. 12 months

Wheel Quiz
a. South and East Africa

Page 14
Find the Difference

Page 15
Zebra Shadow

Wheel Quiz
c. Low

Page 16
Emu Hidden Fact
The emu's egg varies in color from black to dark green. The shell is very thick.

Wheel Quiz
c. Up to 6.6 feet.

Page 18
What Does It Mean?
a. An animal with a pouch

Page 19
Match the kangaroo

Wheel Quiz
a. Grass and leaves

Page 20
Word Maze

Page 21
Wombat Shadow

Wheel Quiz
b. Grass and roots

Page 22
Quiz
1. b; 2. c; 3. c; 4. a; 5. b;
6. b; 7. b; 8. a; 9. a; 10. c

Page 24
Pronghorn Code Breaker
The pronghorn is not an antelope.

Page 25
Spot the difference

Wheel Quiz
c. North America

Page 26
Bison Shadows

Page 27
Label the picture

Wheel Quiz
b. Up to 11.5 feet

Page 28
Word Search

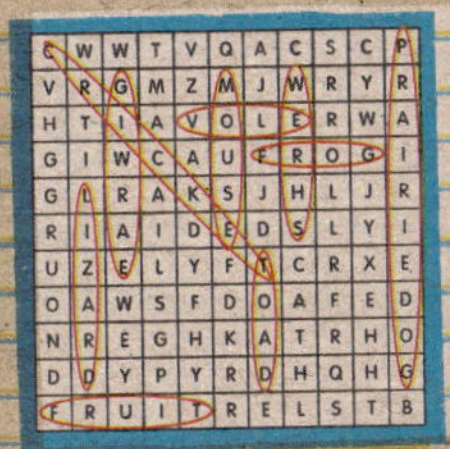

Page 29
Calculator Code
HORSE, COW, DUNG

Wheel Quiz
c. Low

Page 30
Prairie Dog Maze

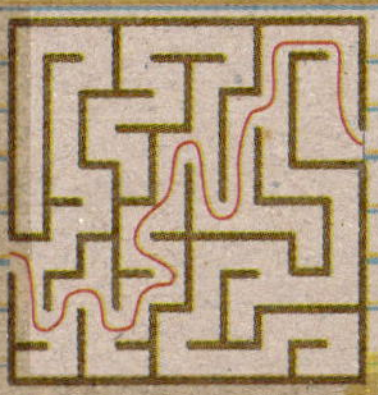

Page 31
Hidden Food
There are 18 grasshoppers

Wheel Quiz
a. Grass and insects

Page 32
Close-Up

Page 33
How Many?
There are 16 snakes

Wheel Quiz
b. Medium

Page 34
Odd One Out

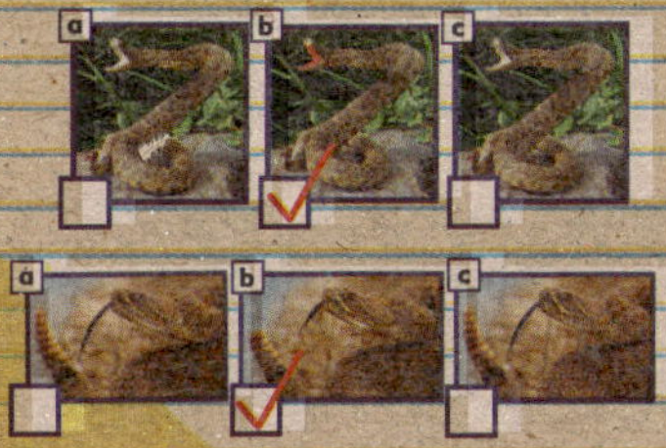

Wheel Quiz
c. Up to 4 feet

Page 36
Wild Dog Maze

Page 37
Spot the Difference

Wheel Quiz
c. Wildebeest, zebra, antelope

Page 38
Follow the Trail
Trail b.

Page 39
Label the Picture

Wheel Quiz
b. Medium

Page 40
Code Breaker
BORN; CUB; SPOTTED; FADES; SIX

Page 41
Spot the Difference

Wheel Quiz
b. 8 feet

Page 42
Shadows

Page 43
Hidden Message
Africa

Wheel Quiz
b. Medium

Page 44

Page 45
Giraffe = Acacia leaves
Elephant = Seed pods
Cougar = Deer
Pronghorn = Cacti
Wild dog = Zebra

Credits/ Acknowledgments

b = bottom, t = top, r = right, l = left, c = center

Front cover b Getty/Martin Harvey, c Getty/Martin Harvey, r Getty/DEA/C.Dani-I.Jeske. Inside front cover t Getty/Martin Ruegner, bl Getty/Steve & Ann Toon, br Getty/Matthias Clamer

Back cover Getty/Gail Shotlander

Wheel front, clockwise from red kangaroo: istockphoto/Hogo, istockphoto/Keiichi Hiki, Getty/Joel Sartore, istockphoto/Robert Hardholt, Corbis, istockphoto/ Markus Seidel, Dreamstime/ Stephen Meese, istockphoto/ Adrian Assalve, istockphoto/Eric Isselée, istockphoto/John Carnemolla. Wheel reverse, clockwise from prairie snake: istockphoto/Steve Mcsweeny, istockphoto/ Peter Malsbury, istockphoto/ Vladimir Titarenko, istockphoto/ Anna Yu, istockphoto/Wolfgang Steiner, istockphoto/ Rich Phalin, istockphoto/ Eric Foltz, istockphoto/ Jill Fromer, istockphoto/ Mark Lundborg, istockphoto/ Michael Zurawski. 1 istockphoto/Svetlana Starostina, 2 and 3 Getty/Joel Sartore, 4 istockphoto/Britta Kasholm-Tengve, 5 istockphoto/Chris Fourie, 6 istockphoto/Neal McClimon, 7t istockphoto/Keith Barlow, 7b istockphoto/Eric Isselée, 8 istockphoto/Markus Seidel, 9 istockphoto/Svetlana Starostina, 10t istockphoto/Eric Isselée, 10b istockphoto/Tobias Helbig, 11t istockphoto/Anders Aagesen, 11 istockphoto/Adrian Assalve, 12 istockphoto/Johan Swanepoel, 14t istockphoto/Liz Leyden, 14bl istockphoto/Eric Isselée, 15 istockphoto/Eric Isselée, 16 istockphoto/John Carnemolla, 18bl istockphoto, 18br istockphoto/Jan Gottwald, 19 istockphoto/Dirk Freder, 20 istockphoto/William Bullimore, 21 istockphoto/Keiichi Hiki, 25 istockphoto, 26 istockphoto/Eric Isselée, 27t istockphoto/Michael Thompson, 27c istockphoto/Justin Kral, 28 istockphoto/ Jill Fromer, 29 istockphoto/Robert Blanchard, 30 istockphoto/Mark Lundborg, 31 Tomasz Zachariasz, 32 istockphoto/ Michael Zurawski, 33 istockphoto/Maria Dryfhout, 33bl Dreamstime/Stephen McSweeny, 34t istockphoto/Maria Dryfhout, 34b Dreamstime/Stephen McSweeny, 36t istockphoto/Lee Pettet, 36b istockphoto/Peter Malsbury, 38t istockphoto/Joshua Haviv, 38b istockphoto/jason crader, 39 istockphoto/Vladimir Titarenko, 40t istockphoto/Eric Isselée, 40b istockphoto/Eric Isselée, 41 istockphoto/Eric Isselée, 42 istockphoto/Peter Malsbury, 43 istockphoto/Bruce Block

Font: Hotel Coral Essex by Pennyzine / Jason Ramirez.

Written by Cathy Jones

Consultant Gerald Legg

First published by Parragon in 2010

Parragon
Queen Street House
4 Queen Street
Bath BA1 1HE, UK

ISBN 978-1-4075-9269-5

Printed in Malaysia